Snow Dogs
COLORING BOOK
BY: CAMEO ANDERSON & DESIREE JOY

Special Thanks: Gandalf & Mischeif (our own snowdogs) for inspiration. Our nephews, Cartiér, Kashé, Atreyu, & Ezra for encouragement and for keeping our inner children alive.

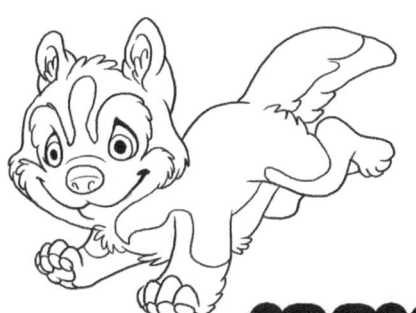

Note: *Each image is on its own page so they can be torn out and gifted, framed, stuck to a refridgerator, turned into a cute paper airplane and to keep markers from bleeding through.*

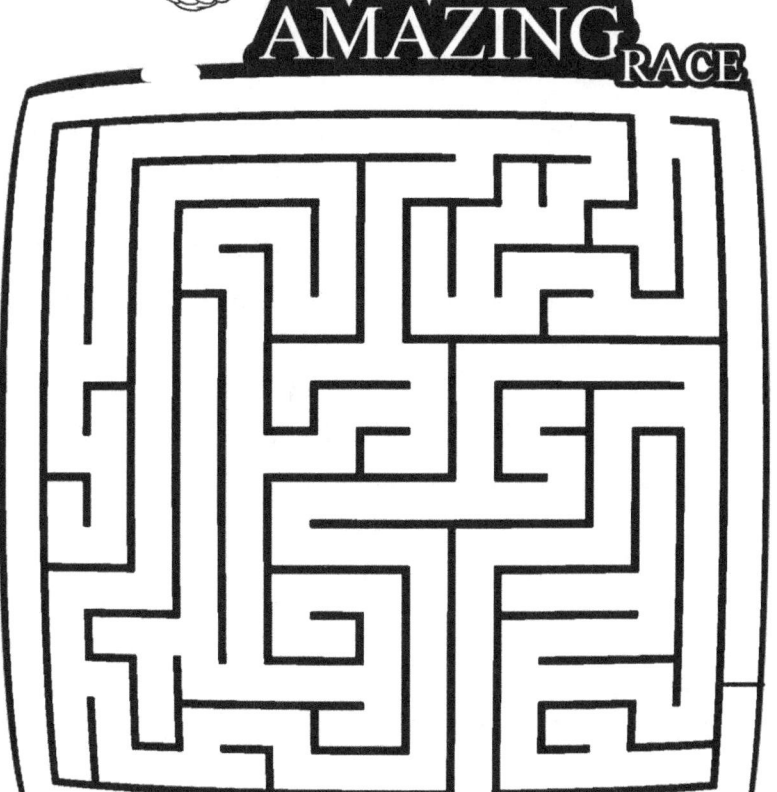

AMAZING RACE

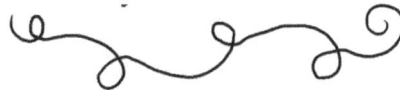

Jenna wants to get to run away and join a sled dog racing team. Help her find her way to Alaska!

Snow Dogs
ROCK

LOVE SNOW DOGS? WANT ONE? ADOPT!

HUNDREDS are killed in shelters every year. Save a life, make a friend, make a difference. Here are some fine agencies who offer snow dogs in need of homes.

---

http://www.alleysrescuedangels.org/

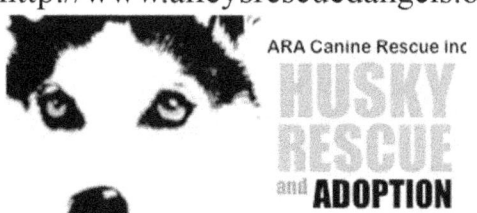

ARA Canine Rescue inc
HUSKY RESCUE and **ADOPTION**

Adoption Line: 951-532-0491

Email: alleysangels@gmail.com

Mailing address: ARA Canine Rescue inc., 15555 Main Street. #D4-188. HESPERIA. CA 92345

http://www.huskyrescue.org/

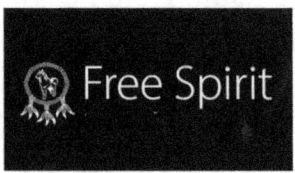

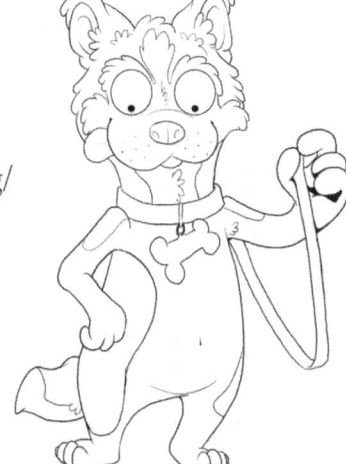

FOREVER HUSKY
http://foreverhusky.org/

HUSKY HOUSE
www.huskyhouse.org/

Hairy Houdini Husky Rescue
www.hhshr.com/

Texas Sled Dog Rescue
www.texassleddogrescue.org/

Husky Haven
huskyhaven.org/

Northern Lights Sled Dog Rescue
http://awos.petfinder.com/shelters/northernlights.html

Taysia Blue Siberian Husky Rescue
https://www.taysiablue.com/

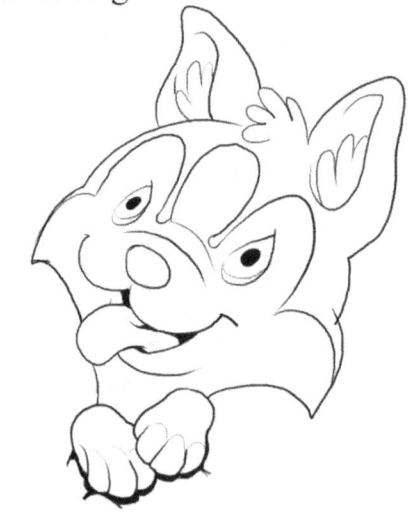

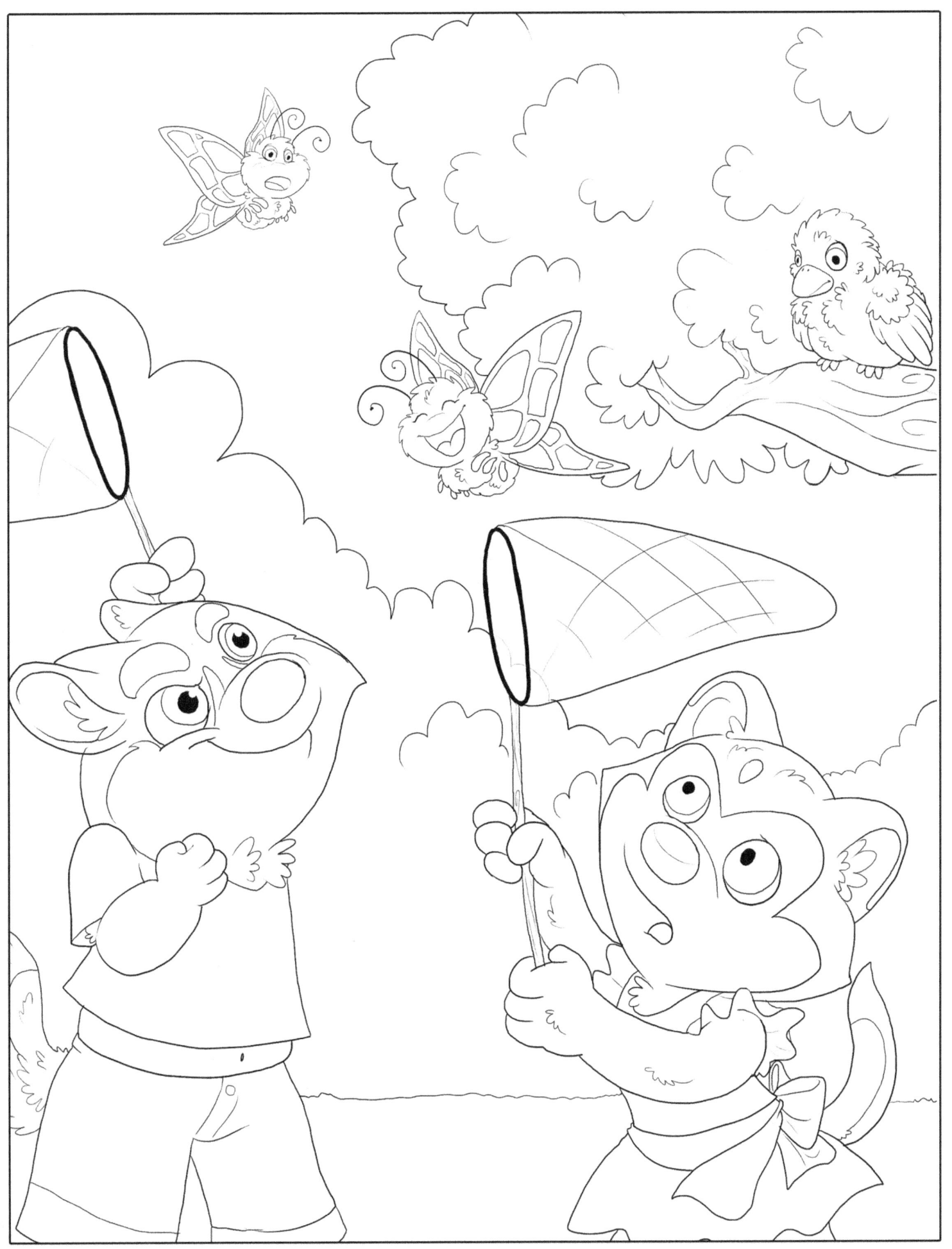

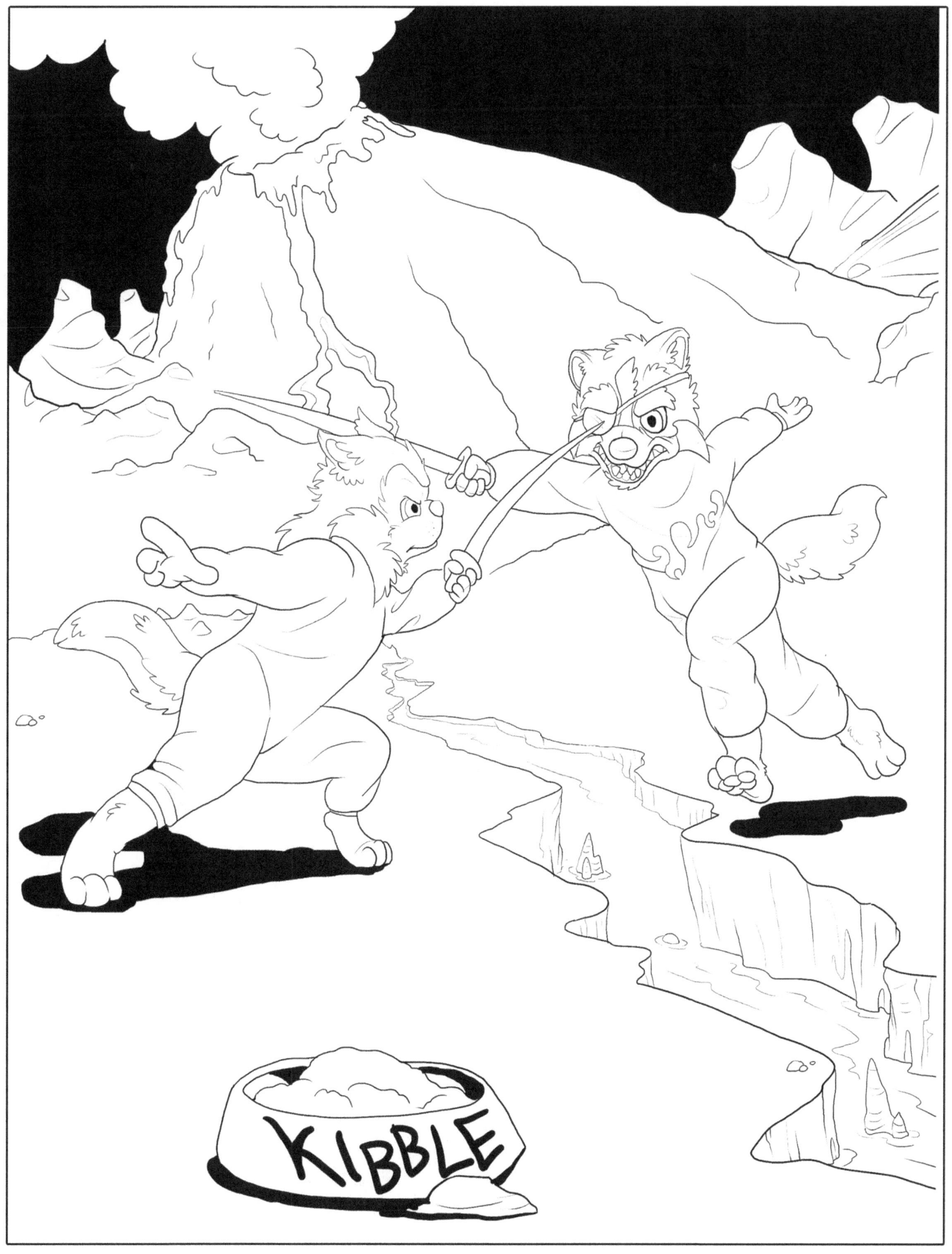

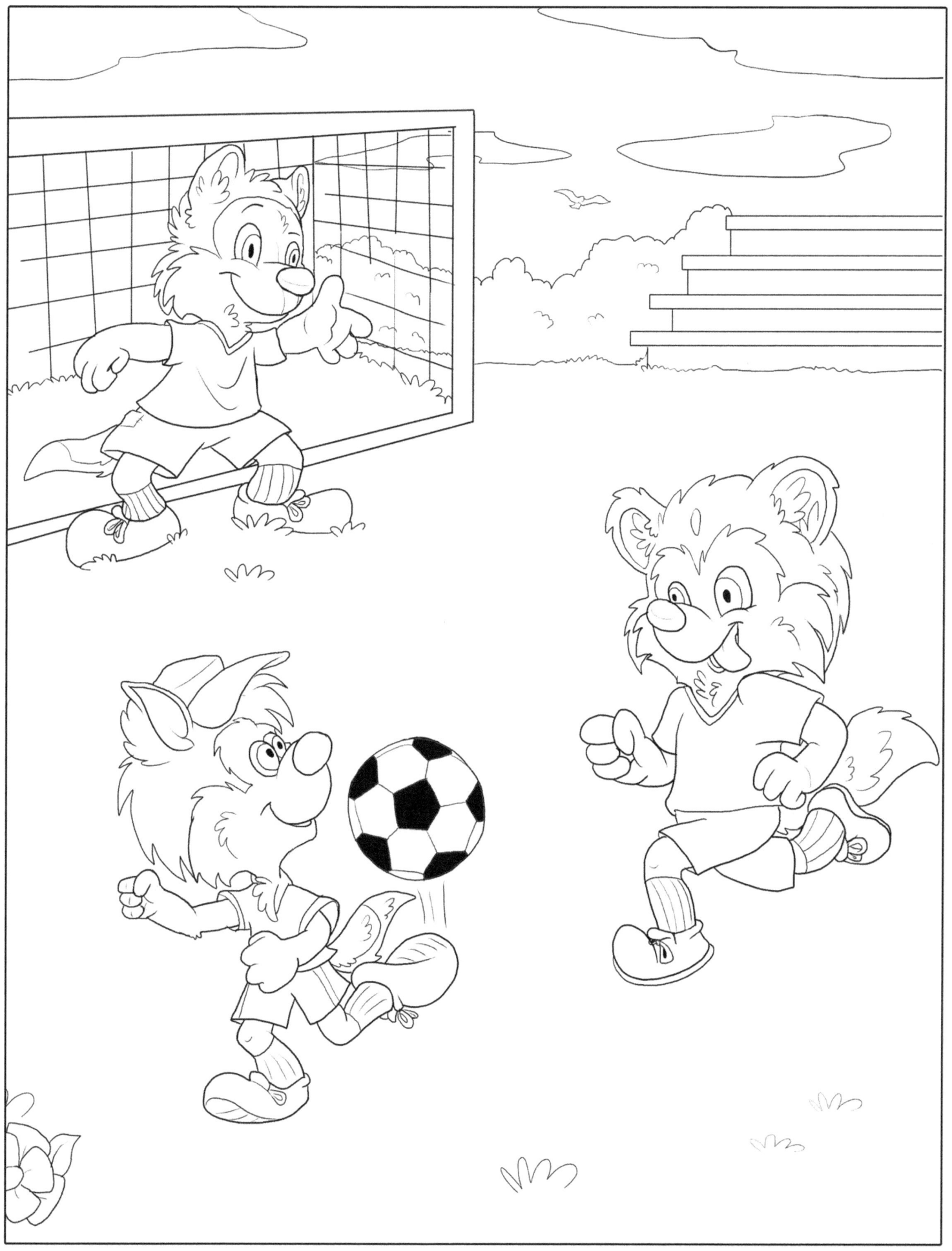

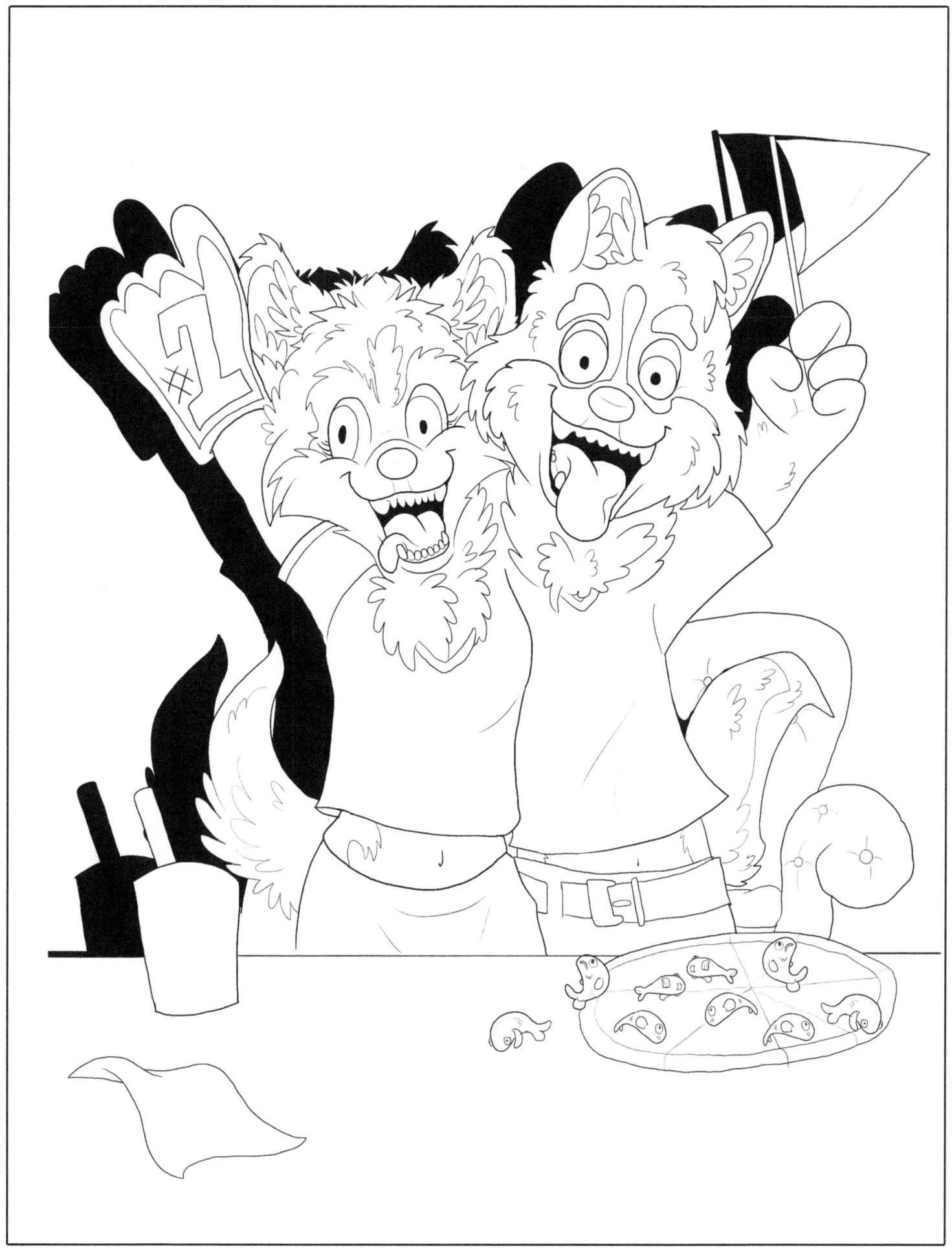

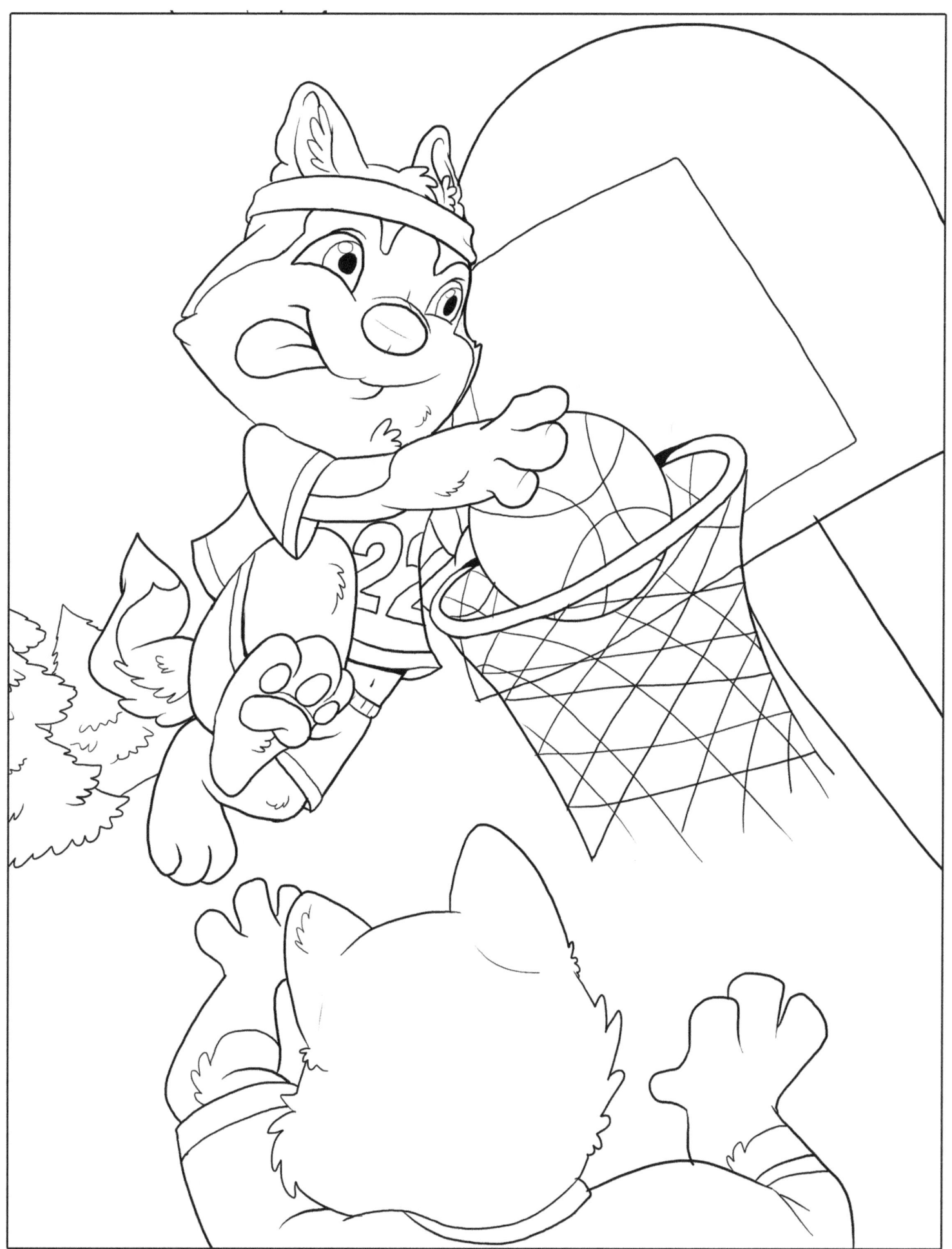

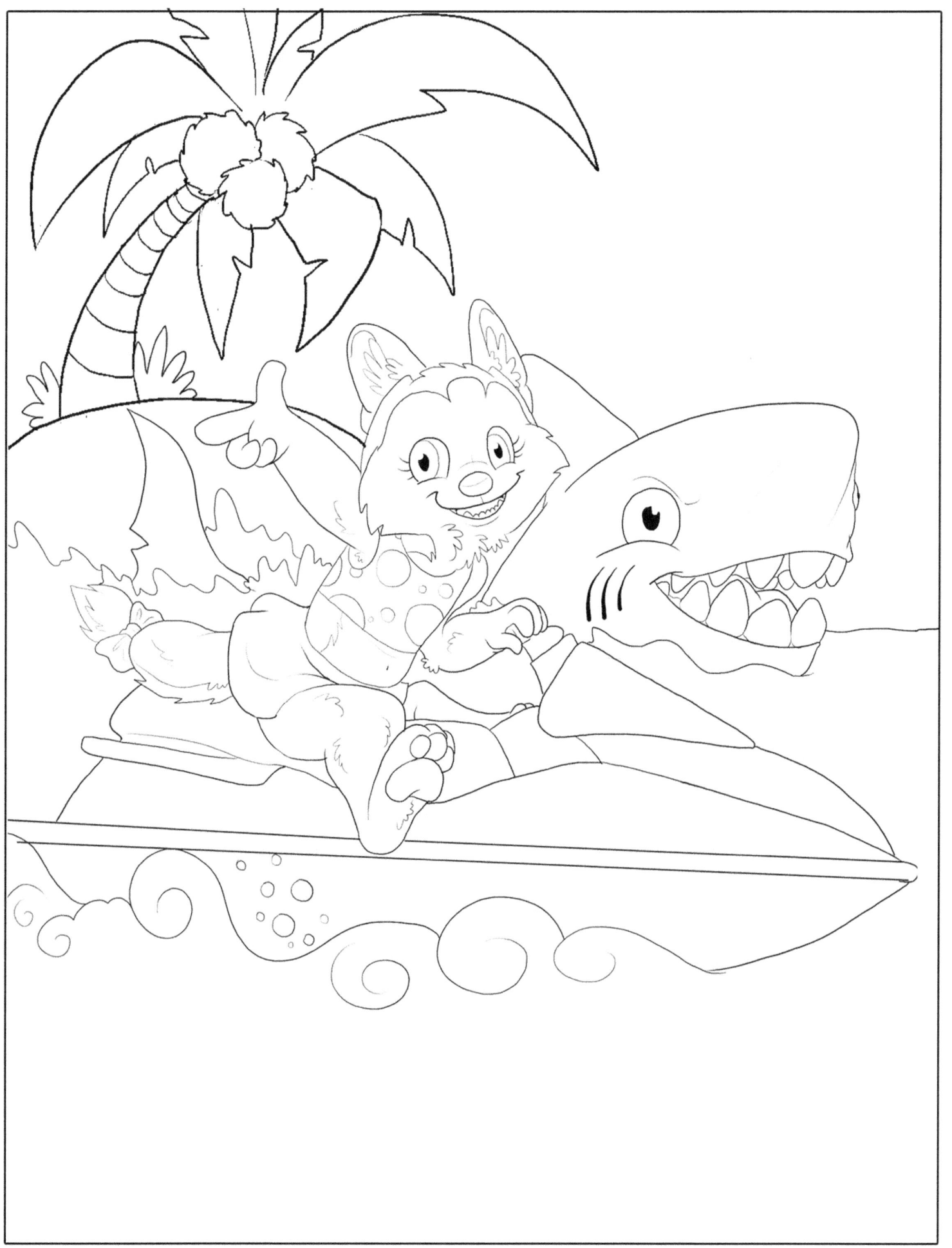

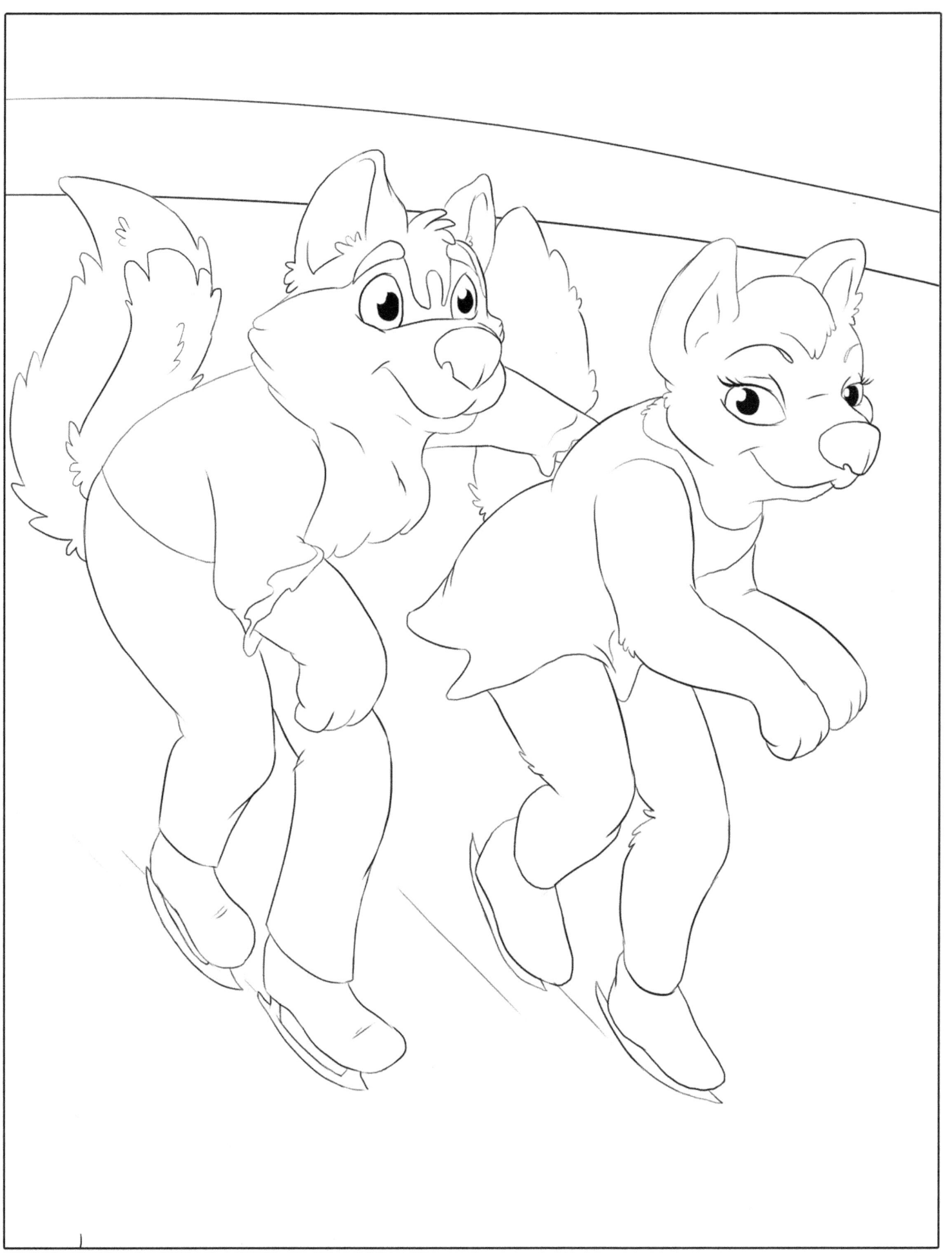

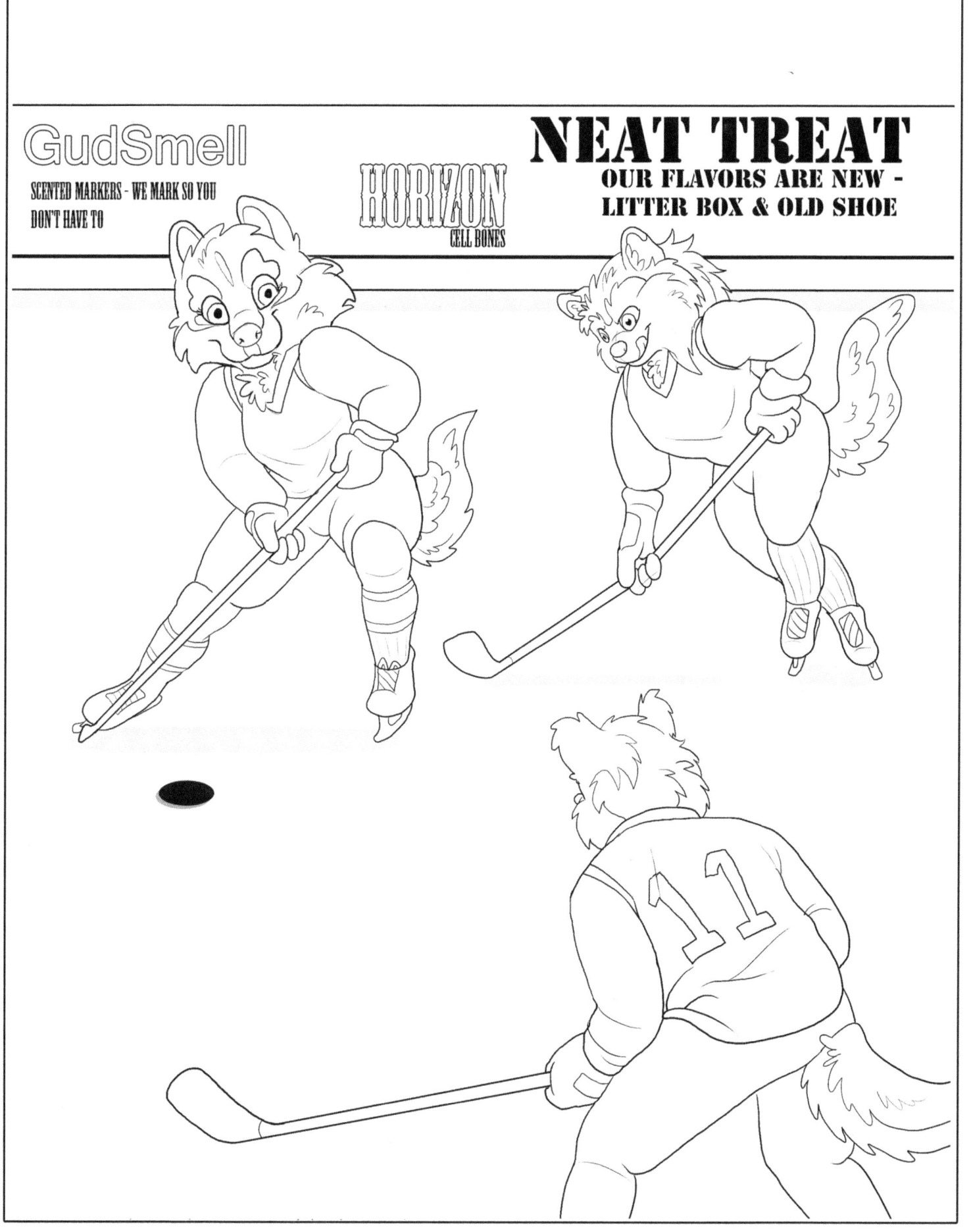

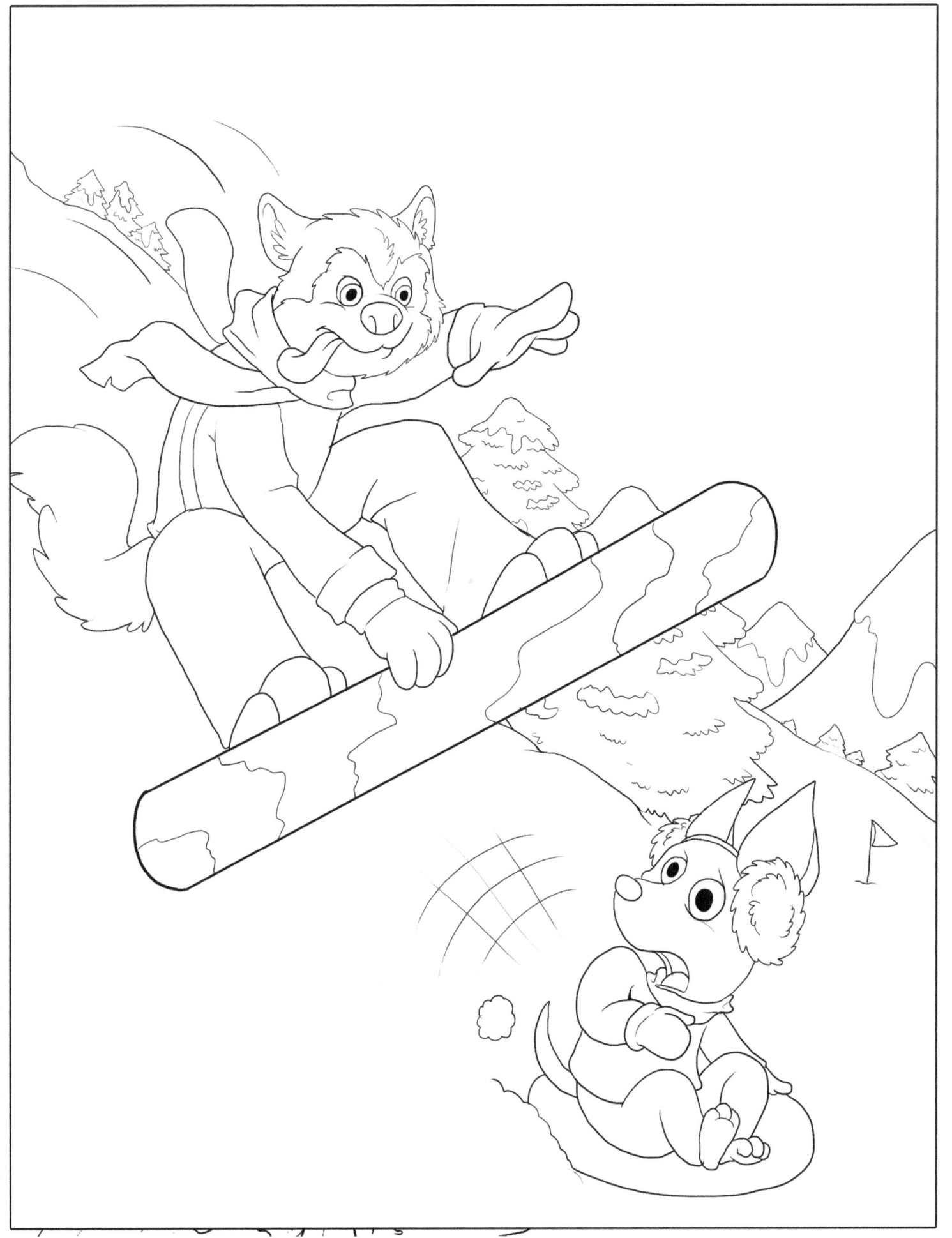

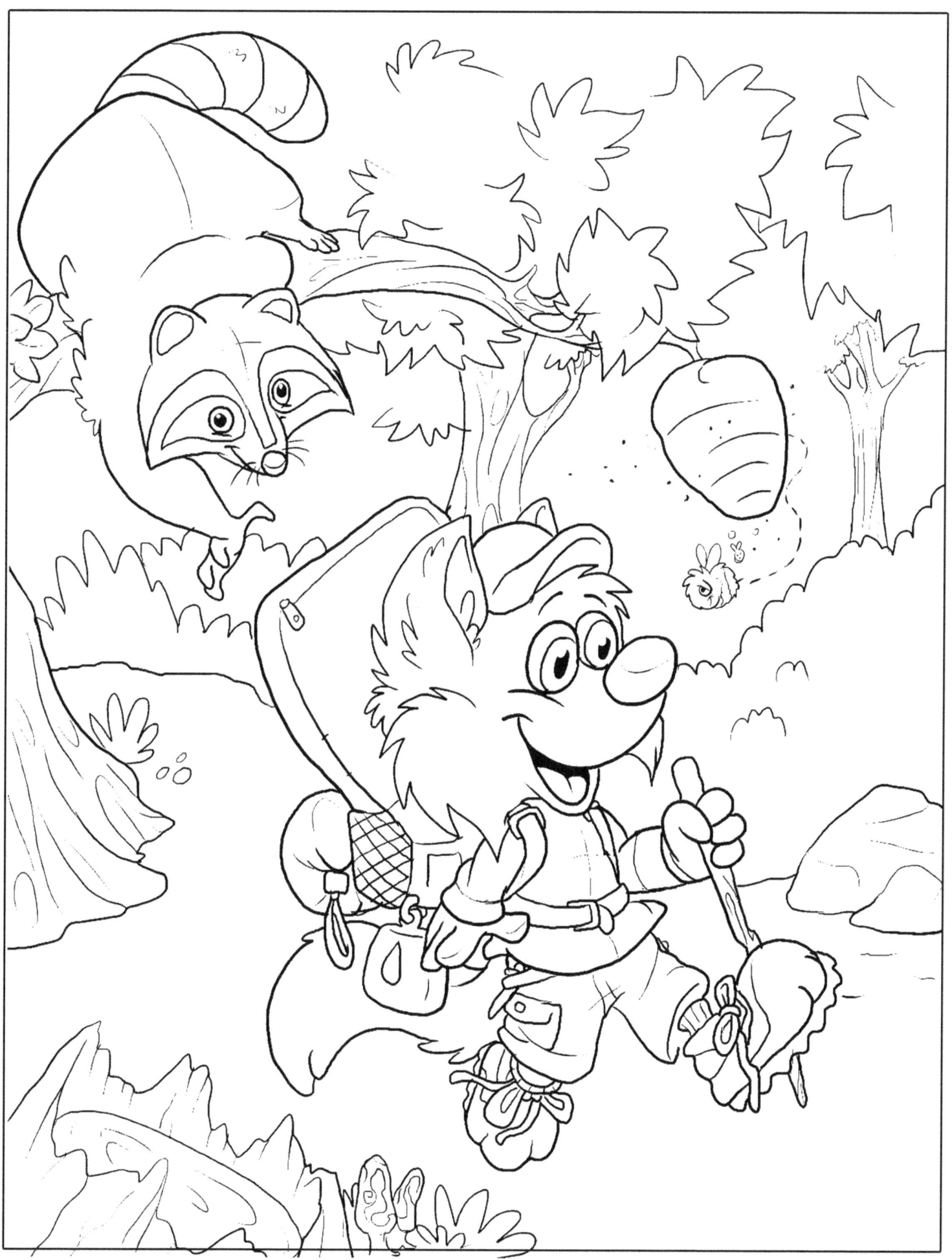

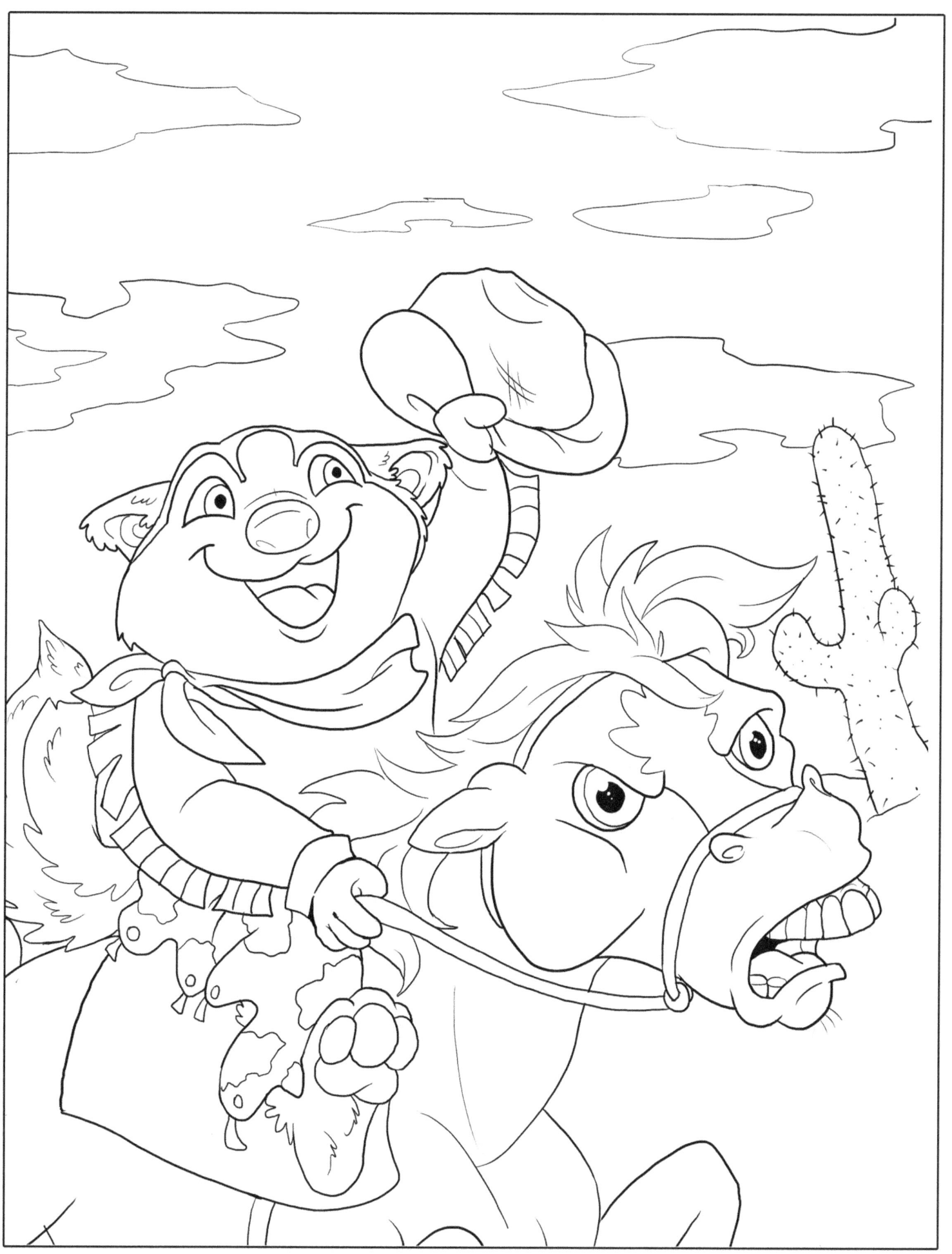

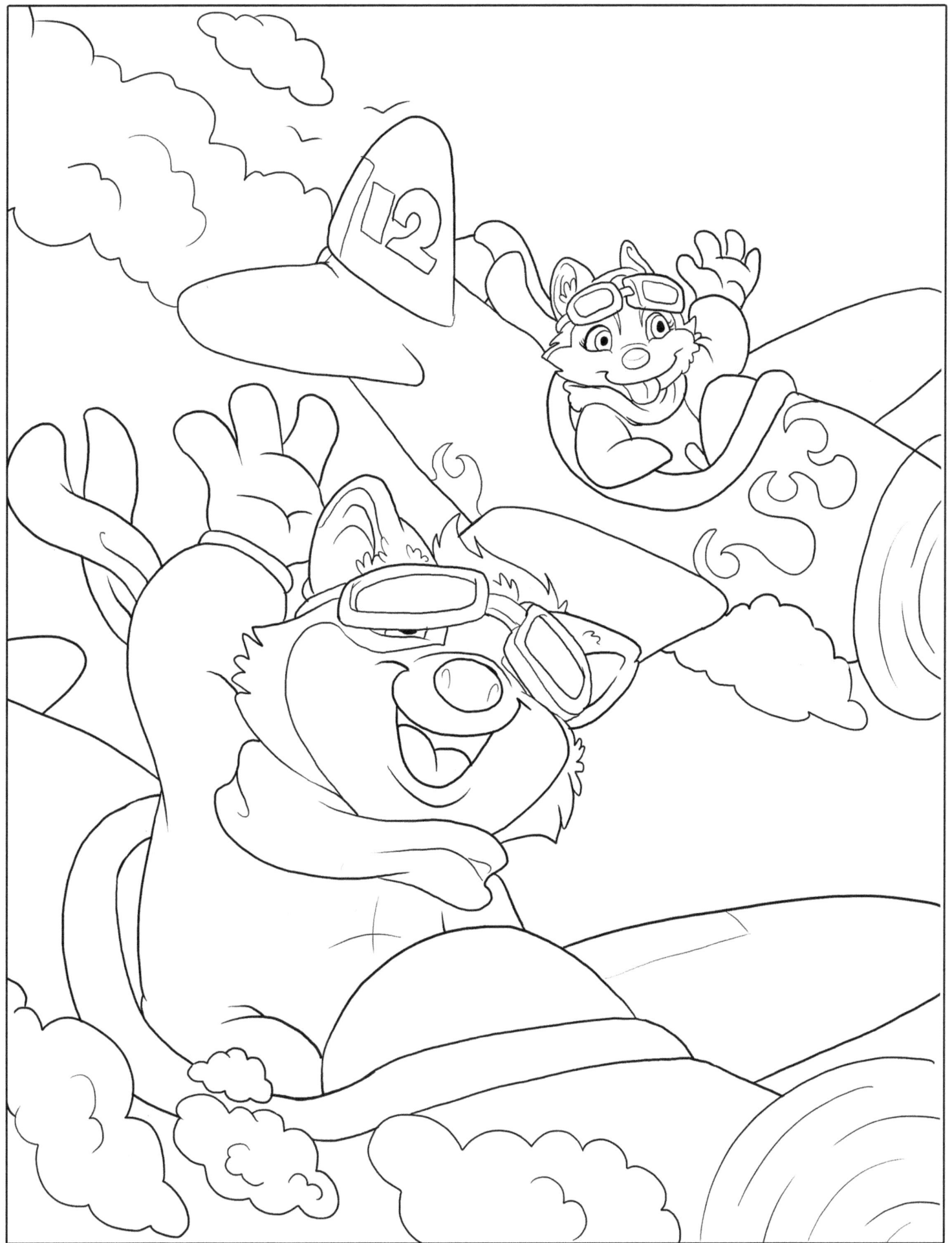

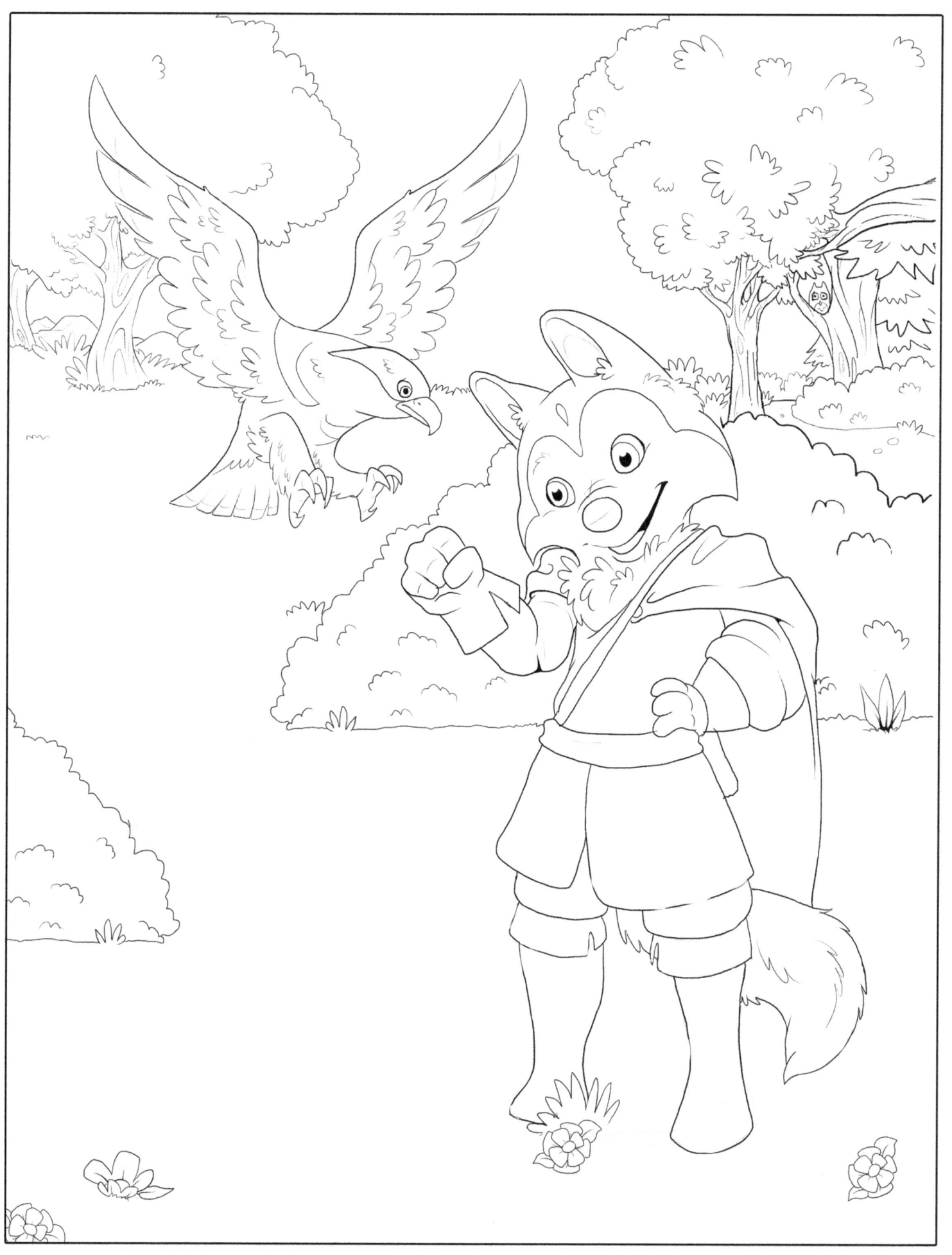

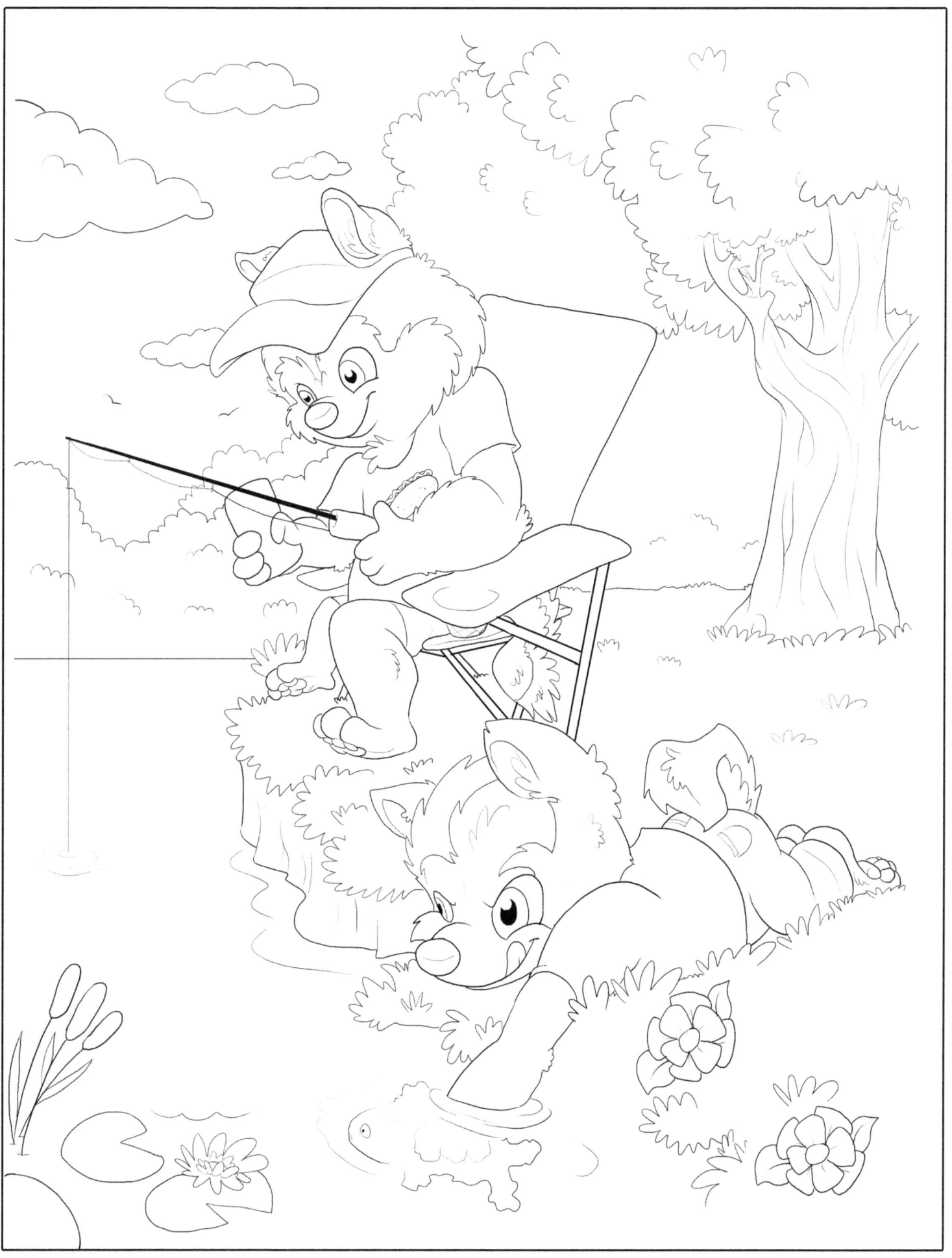

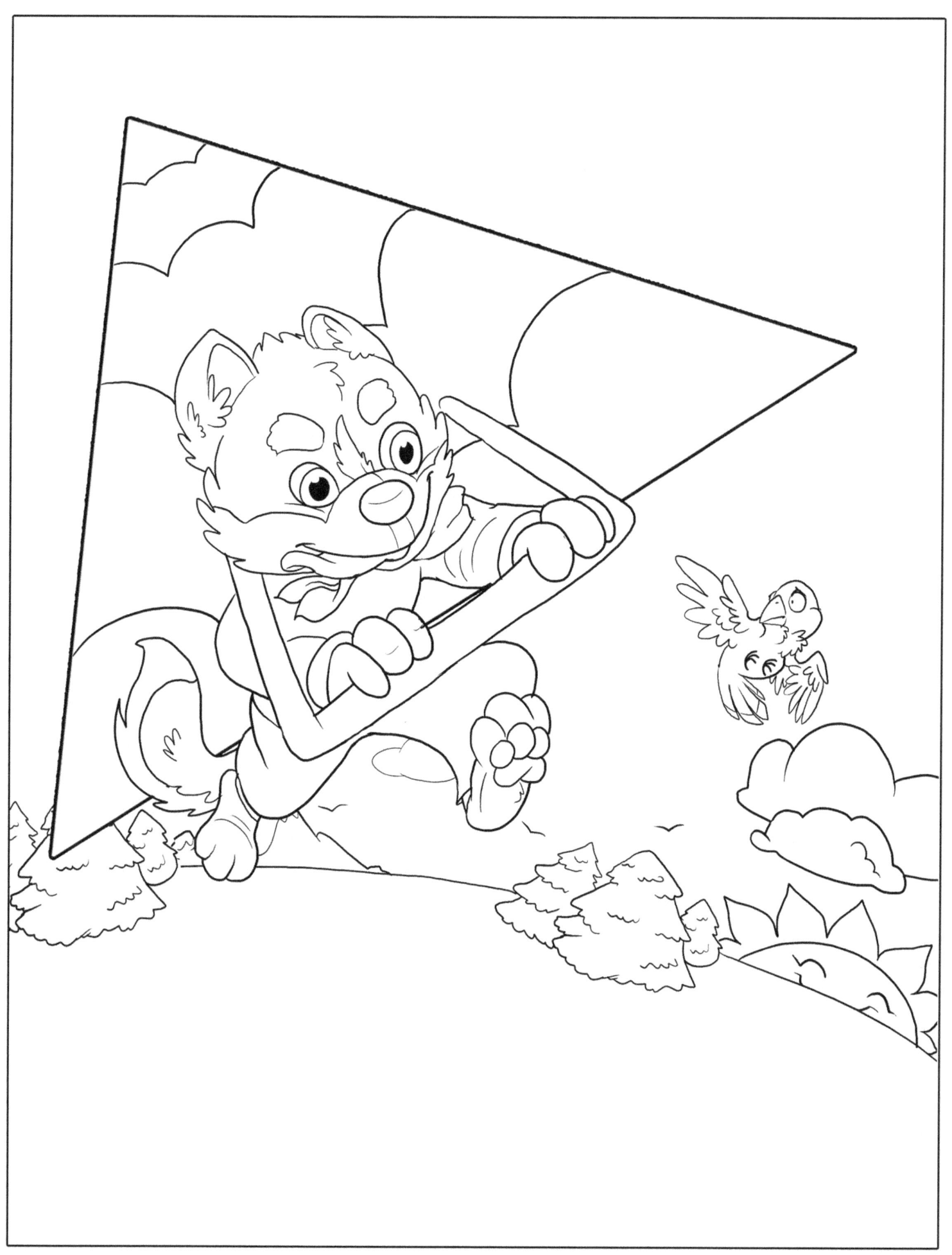

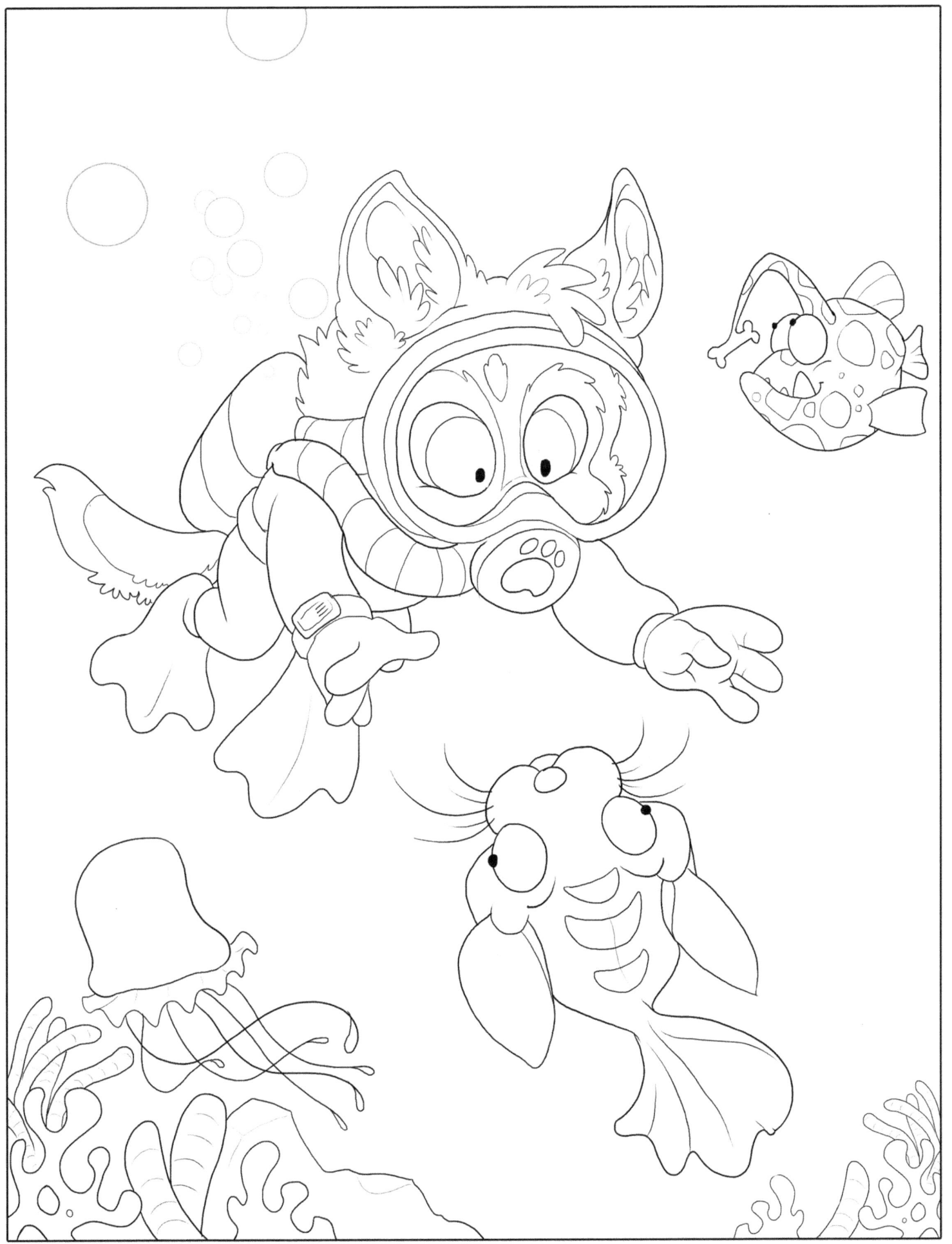

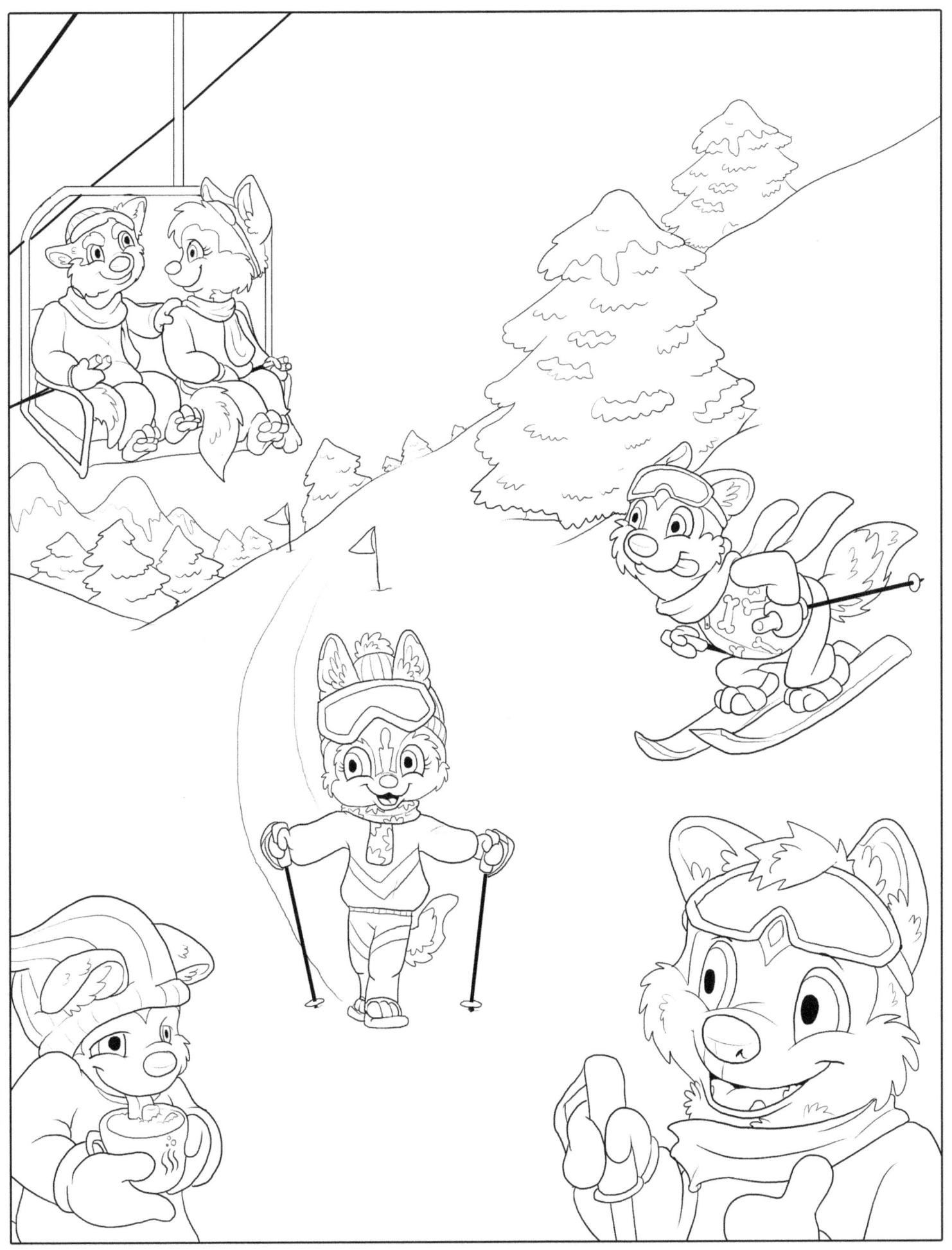

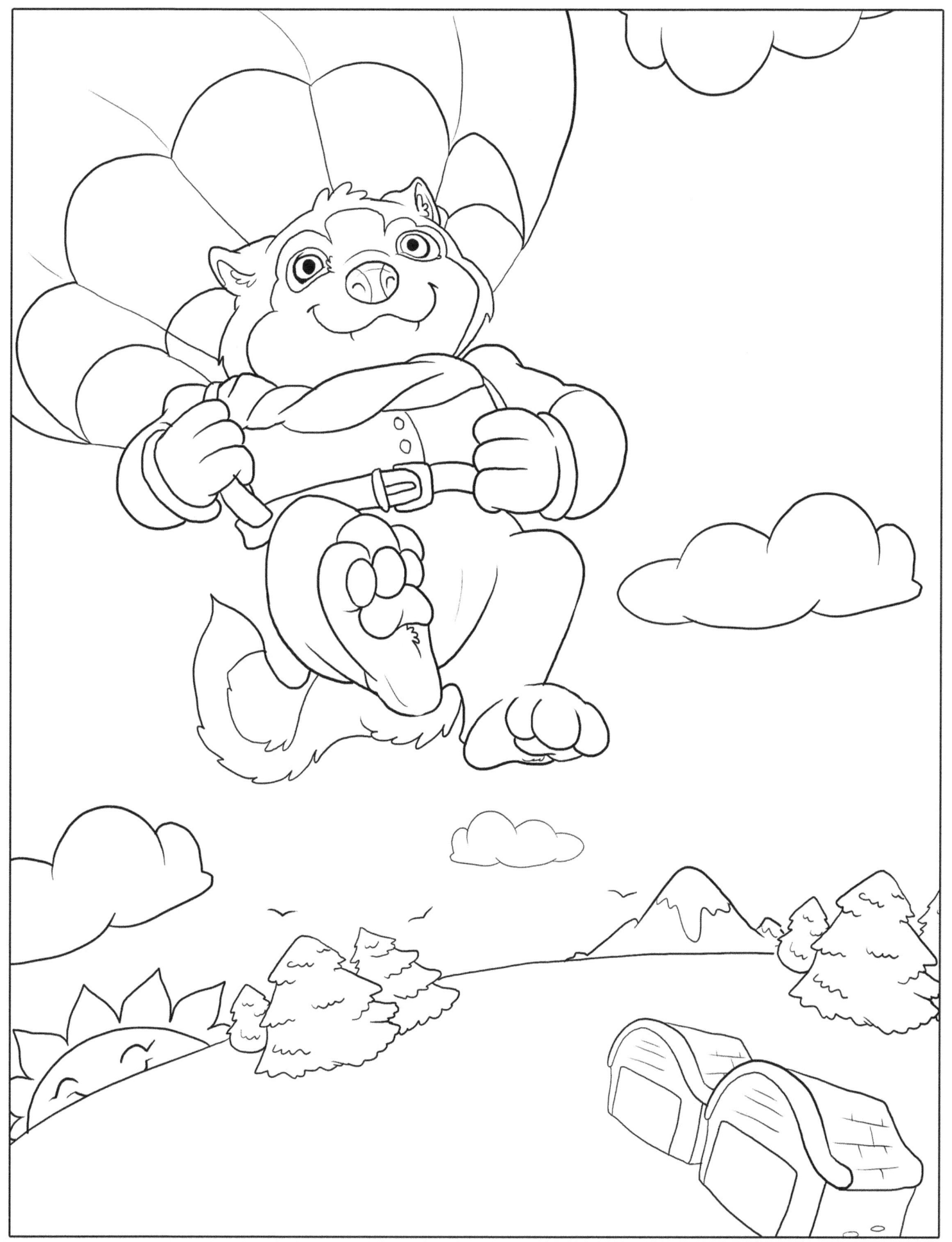

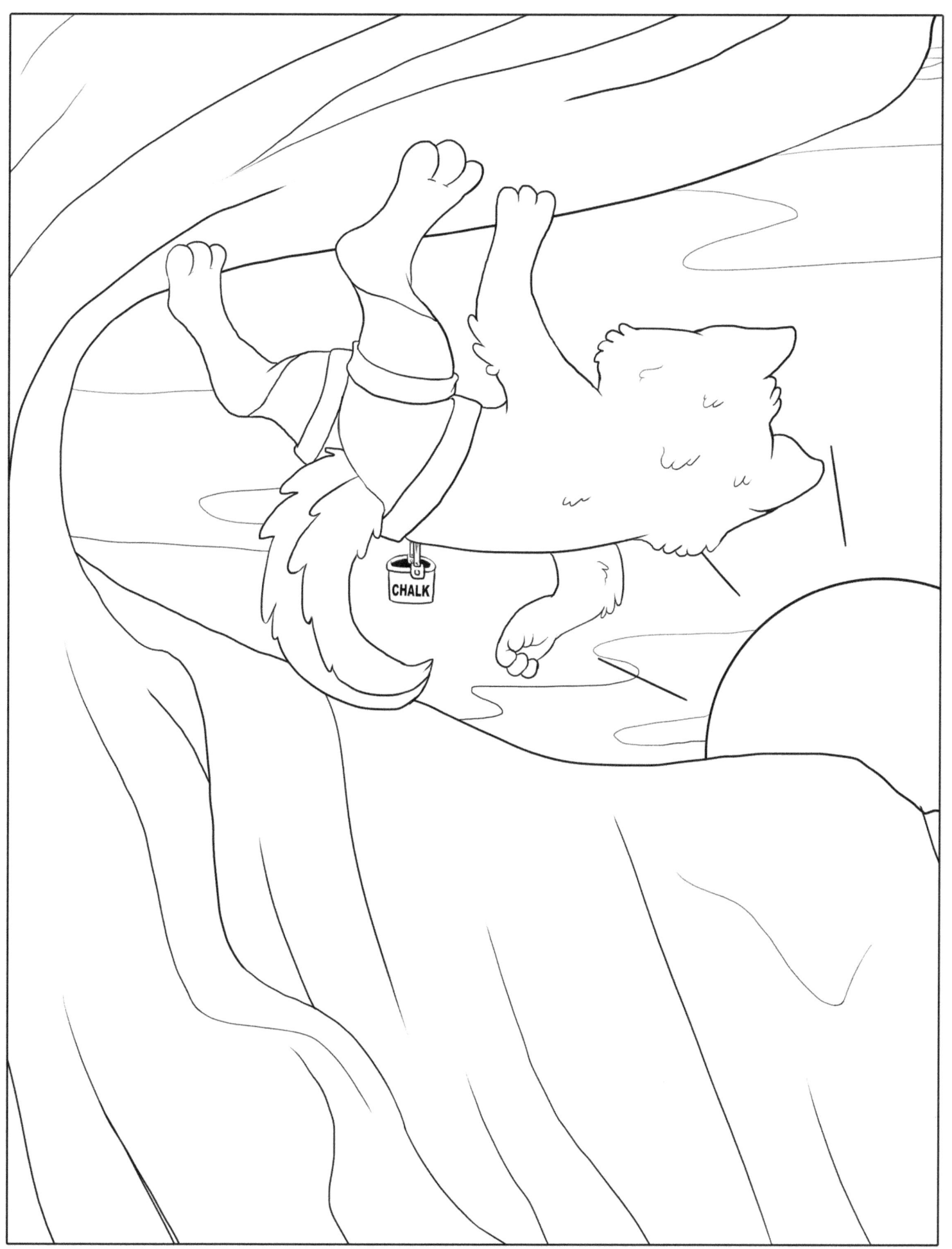

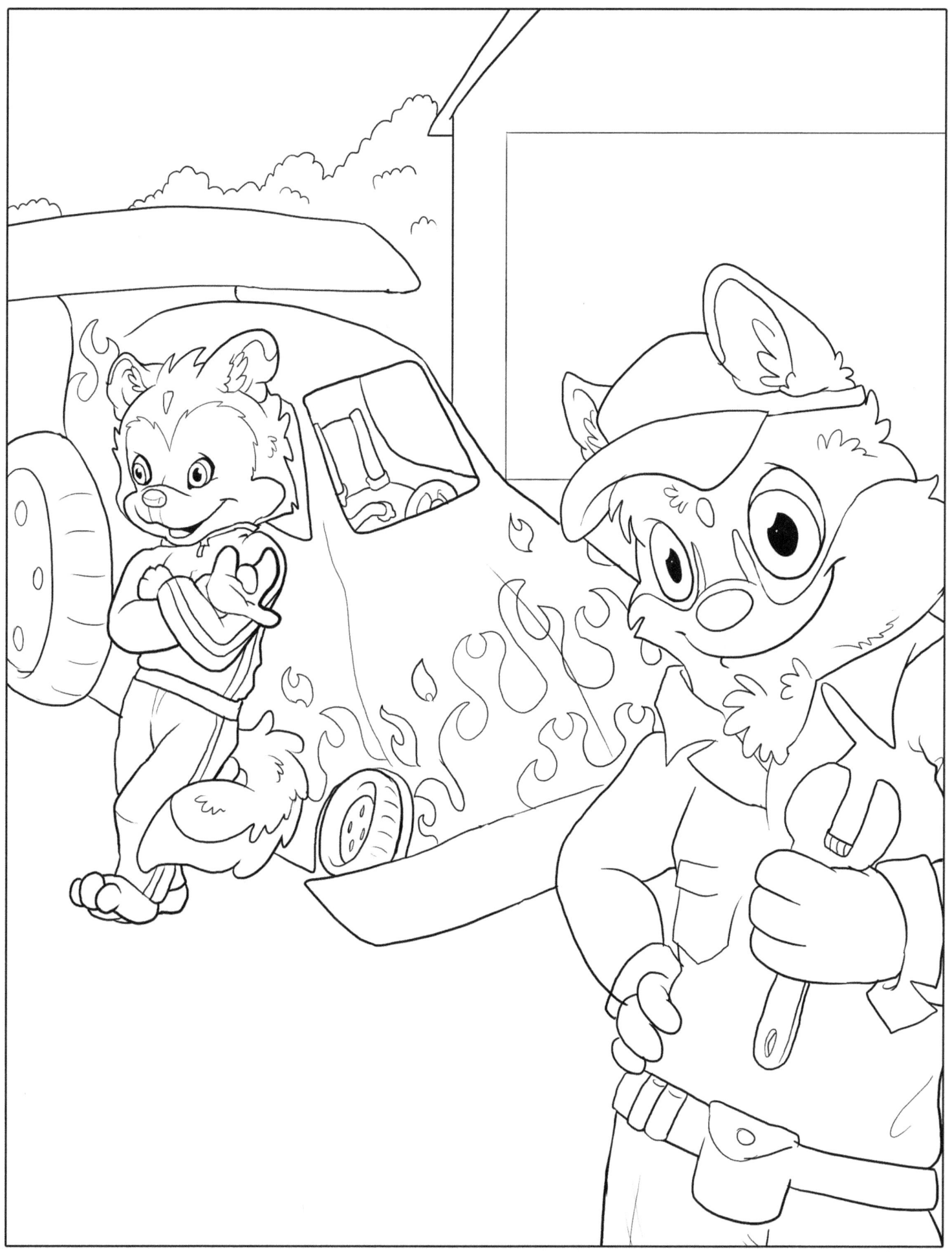

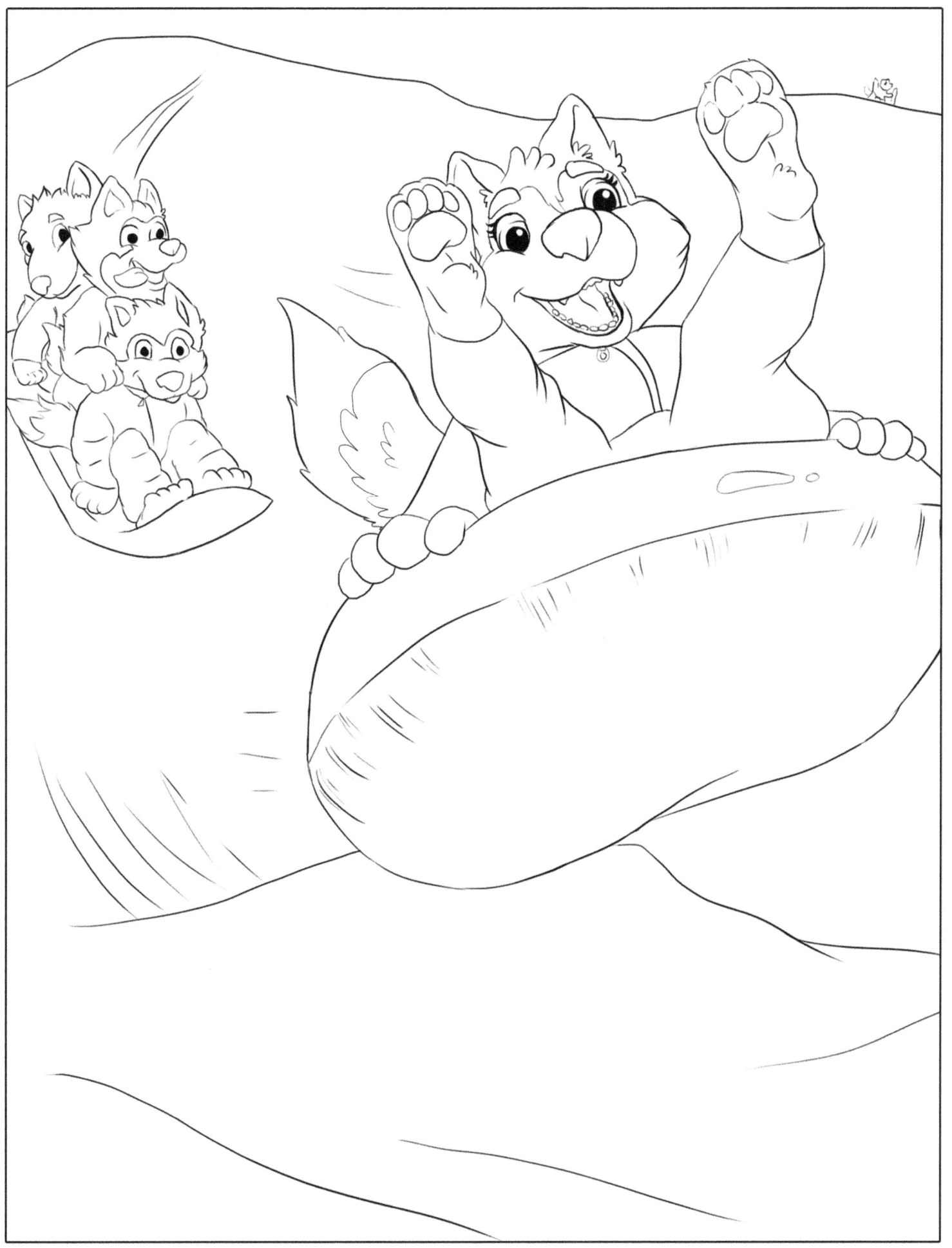

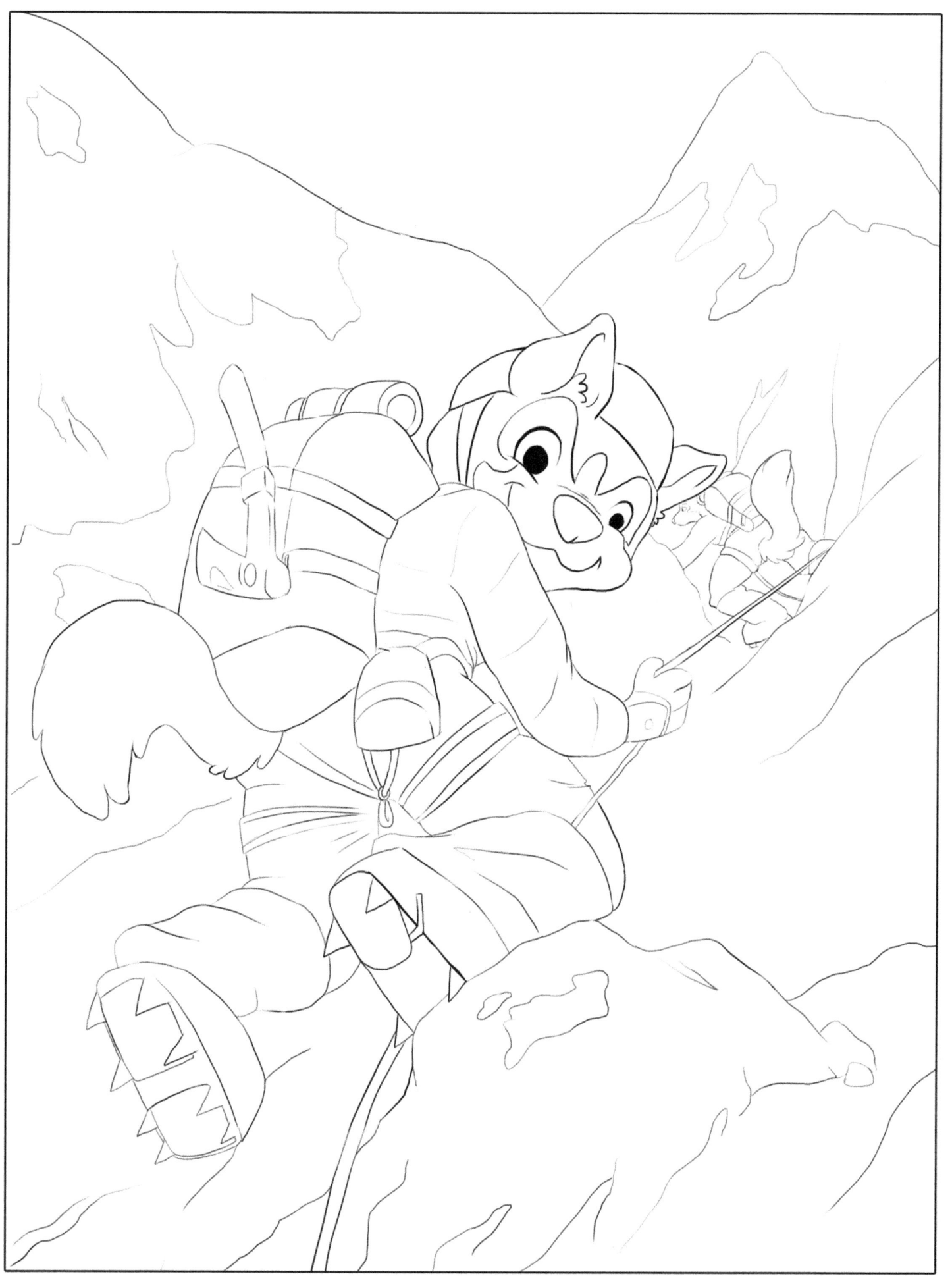

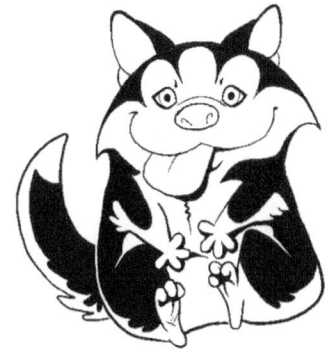

I CAN TAKE A LICKING
By: Cameo Anderson

Living by yourself can take a toll upon your health,
So get yourself a dog from a rescue catalog.
A pup that's big or little, if you'll excuse a little spittle,
Will brighten up your day with a lot of love and play.
A tickling lick cures sadness quick,
Erases sick, and makes smiles stick.
A hyper little licker can heal a broken ticker,
make your love grow thicker and end sadness a bit quicker.
Even a calm old fellow who is just a little mellow,
will share enough slime to make you happy all the time.
So if you're tired of work or school,
get a dog who likes to drool and from that day your life will rule!

DIGGING FOR DICTION
how many snow-dog words can you find?

T	I	P	U	P	K	A	U	R	O	R	A	N	A	D
A	S	C	F	U	L	O	Y	A	L	H	O	W	L	I
I	D	A	I	L	E	H	R	A	C	E	L	O	N	K
L	N	O	M	L	E	U	K	A	N	A	W	R	I	R
I	U	S	A	A	K	S	N	O	W	D	O	G	S	O
F	O	G	N	W	A	K	I	T	A	G	O	E	I	W
T	H	A	I	L	I	Y	T	T	G	A	N	E	B	R
O	K	R	A	C	S	L	E	D	O	T	E	M	E	E
D	L	D	R	O	K	I	D	A	N	E	P	E	T	S
N	E	L	S	M	A	L	A	M	U	T	E	S	S	C
O	F	Y	L	E	T	E	C	A	R	M	U	S	H	U
M	U	E	O	A	H	A	W	A	L	K	G	H	E	E
E	R	L	V	M	N	D	I	G	M	C	O	L	D	V
N	O	P	E	N	A	L	O	P	A	I	C	E	Z	A
W	I	N	T	E	R	S	M	E	L	L	S	K	I	N

Write all the words you find in this box:

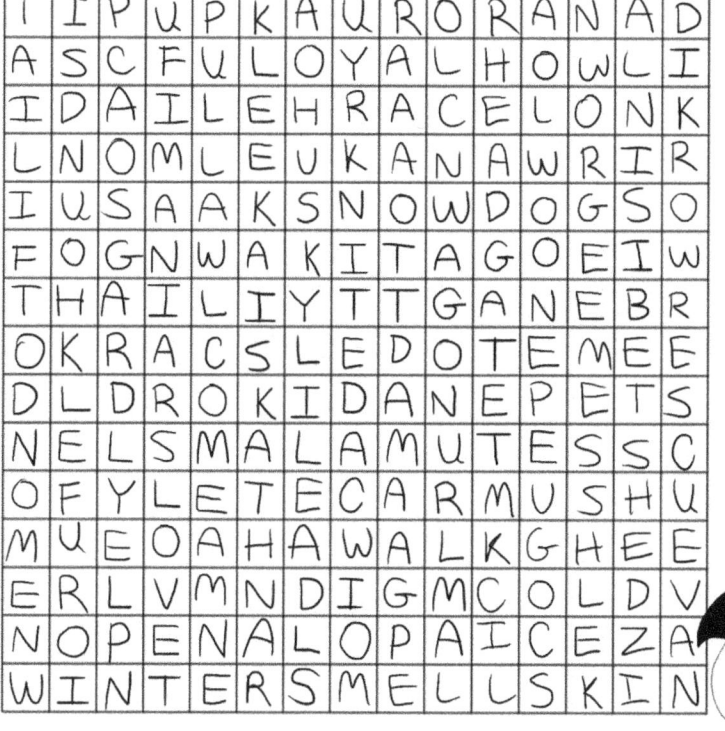

www.ingramcontent.com/pod-product-compliance
Lightning Source LLC
Chambersburg PA
CBHW080609190526

45169CB00007B/2941

* 9 7 8 1 5 3 3 1 0 4 7 6 2 *